DRIVE THRU

THE STORY OF
SUGAR

By Shalini Vallepur

THE COOKIE JAR

BEARPORT
PUBLISHING

Minneapolis, Minnesota

Credits

All images are courtesy of Shutterstock.com, unless otherwise specified.
With thanks to Getty Images, Thinkstock Photo and iStockphoto.

Front Cover images - mir_vam, asantosg, brgfx, picoStudio. Recurring images -
Flas100, Alfmaler, Alter-ego, Iamkaoo99, IMissisHope, mir_vam, NikitaRoytman
Photography, asantosg, brgfx, Cool Vector Make, picoStudio, olllikeballoon. 4&5 -
Incomible. 6&7 - Alf Ribeiro, Ekkaratk, Luis Carlos Jimenez del rio. 8&9 - BLAGORODEZ,
javarman, TB studio. 10&11 - Jackson Stock Photography, TORWAISTUDIO. 12&13 - Johan
Larson, Ultrakwang. 14&15 - A-Nurak, BigMouse, mailsonpignata. 16&17 - Hywit Dimyadi,
Matyas Rehak. 18&19 - Apirak Rungrueang, iPreech Studio, Nataliia Zhekova. 20&21 -
Lukiyanova Natalia frenta, CK Bangkok Photography, David Cardinez, neelsky, stocktr,
Vicky Jirayu, Yavuz Sariyildiz. 22&23 - Hein Nouwens, Mathee saengkaew, Anatolir.

Library of Congress Cataloging-in-Publication Data

Names: Vallepur, Shalini, author.
Title: The story of sugar / by Shalini Vallepur.
Description: Fusion edition. | Minneapolis, MN : Bearport Publishing
    Company, [2021] | Series: Drive thru | Includes bibliographical
    references and index.
Identifiers: LCCN 2020010632 (print) | LCCN 2020010633 (ebook) | ISBN
    9781647473259 (library binding) | ISBN 9781647473303 (paperback) | ISBN
    9781647473358 (ebook)
Subjects: LCSH: Sugar–Juvenile literature.
Classification: LCC TX560.S9 V35 2021 (print) | LCC TX560.S9 (ebook) |
    DDC 641.3/36–dc23
LC record available at https://lccn.loc.gov/2020010632
LC ebook record available at https://lccn.loc.gov/2020010633

For more information, write to Bearport Publishing, 5357 Penn Avenue South,
Minneapolis, MN 55419. Printed in the United States of America.

CONTENTS

HOP IN THE COOKIE JAR

Hello! I'm Eli, and this is my food truck. It's called the Cookie Jar because I make the sweetest cookies around.

* MENU *

Plain cookie

Frosted cookie

Chocolate chip cookie

Oatmeal cookie

Oh, no! I'm out of sugar! I use sugar to make my cookies. I need to get more sugar. Hop in the Cookie Jar and join me!
THE COOKIE JAR

THE STORY OF SUGAR

Sugar farm in Brazil

Sugar is grown on farms in countries around the world.

THE COOKIE JAR

We get **refined sugar** from two plants called sugarcane and sugar beet.

Sugarcane

Sugar beets

Sugarcane and sugar beets are very different plants, but the sugar inside is exactly the same.

PERFECT WEATHER

Sugarcane is a type of grass. It grows best in areas that are warm and sunny all year round. It needs a lot of rain.

THE COOKIE JAR

Sugar beet grows best in cooler areas.

My sugarcane map shows some of the countries around the world where sugarcane grows.

China

India

ASIA

EUROPE

NORTH AMERICA

Indonesia

Brazil

AFRICA

South Africa

SOUTH AMERICA

Australia

Let's head to Australia and get some sugar!

THE FARM

We made it to the sugar farm. Each row of plants has space around it so the plants have lots of room to grow.

THE COOKIE JAR

Sugarcane grows to about 16 feet (5 m) tall. It takes about a year for sugarcane to grow to its full size.

Can you see how tall the sugarcane is compared to this person?

TIME TO HARVEST

Sugarcane is usually **harvested** and cut into smaller pieces by **machines** called cane harvesters.

THE COOKIE JAR

The smaller pieces are put into a **trailer** and taken away to make sugar.

In some countries, sugarcane is harvested by hand.

While harvesting, farmers leave a little bit of the sugarcane in the ground. New sugarcane grows from these parts.

13

IN THE MILL

The sugarcane is then brought to a **mill**. It is rolled through a special machine. Sugary juice is squeezed out of the cane.

The juice is collected. Dirt and bits of sugarcane are removed from the juice.

What is left of the sugarcane plant is called bagasse (buh-GAS). This can be used as a **fuel**.

FROM SUGAR TO SYRUP

The sugary juice is taken away to be boiled. Boiling the juice removes water and makes a thick syrup.

The sugary juice is being boiled.

The thick syrup is moved into a larger container, where it is boiled again. Sugar crystals begin to form inside the syrup.

Sugar crystals are added to the syrup to help more crystals form during boiling.

The sugar crystals are separated from the thick syrup in a machine that spins very fast.

The syrup turns into something called molasses.

MOLASSES

This leaves us with sugar crystals! The sugar crystals are then cleaned and ground into smaller **granules.**

A WORLD OF SUGAR

It is thought that people have been eating sugar for around 10,000 years! People chewed on sugarcane when they wanted a sweet treat.

SUGARCANE JUICE

A lot of people drink the sweet juice from the sugarcane.

Today, lots of sweet treats are made from sugar.

Sugar is boiled, cooled down, and stretched to form candy sticks.

CANDY STICKS

Macun is a colorful soft candy from Turkey that is wrapped around sticks.

MACUN

COOKIE TIME!

We made it home! Now you know the story of sugar, and I can bake some cookies. Would you like one?

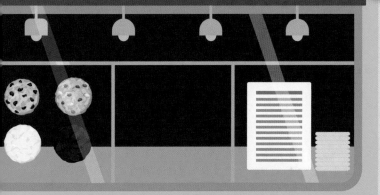

THE COOKIE JAR

* MENU *

Plain cookie

Frosted cookie

Chocolate chip cookie

Oatmeal cookie

Sugary cookies and candies are delicious, but too many can be bad for your teeth! Remember to brush your teeth at least twice a day.

Now you know the story of sugar!

GLOSSARY

fuel something that can be used to make energy or to power something

granules tiny parts of something, such as sugar

harvested when fully grown crops have been picked

machines things with moving parts that do work when given power

mill a building or machine that is used to grind or crush something

refined sugar sugar from sugarcane or sugar beet that is ready to eat

trailer the back part of a truck that carries things

INDEX